ADVANCED

ARABIC

VOCABULARY

HANDBOOK

Zeina Debs Khayat

English -Arabic Advanced
Vocabulary Handbook
Arranged by Topic

Links
Publishing

ISBN 9953 – 488 – 56 – 1

Published and distributed by:

Links Publishing
P.O. Box 145
Stockport SK7 1WJ
United Kingdom
Tel: 0161-2858561
Fax : 0161-2928362
Email : links@khayat.co.uk
Website: www.links-publishing.co.uk

CONTENTS

Foreword

The Advanced Arabic Vocabulary Handbook is a reference guide and revision aid for anyone studying Arabic at a higher level. It is suitable for students taking GCE AS/A level and university students, as well as those learning Arabic for business purposes.

Contemporary words and sentences are arranged in topic-based sections in alphabetical order. Each section provides the user with an up-to-date collection of essential vocabulary, covering five areas of knowledge:
1) Day to day matters
2) Society
3) The working world
4) The environment and citizenship
5) The international context.

The last section includes linking words, prepositions and interrogatives, names of some countries and opening phrases to help with essay, speech and letter writing.

This handbook is also useful for native Arabic speakers wishing to enhance their English vocabulary.

Chapter 1:

Day-to-day matters

Food and diet,
Health,
Transport, travel and tourism,
Current affairs and media.

الفصل الأول

الشؤون اليوميّة

الطعام والشراب،
الصحّة،
وسائل التنقّل والسياحة،
قضايا العصر والإعلام.

FOOD AND DIET

Amount	كميّة	Container	قدر / وعاء
Almonds	لوز	Cooking pot	قدر الطهي
Apple	تفّاح	Corn	ذرة
Apricot	مشمش	Courgette	كوسى
Aubergine	باذنجان	Cream	قشدة
Banana	موز	Cubed	مكعّب
Barley	شعير	Cucumber	خيار
Beans	فول/فاصوليا	Dairy products	مُنتَجات الحليب
Beef	لحم بقر	Delicious food	طعام لذيذ
Beneficial	مفيد	Dessert	حلوى
Bitter	مُرّ	Diet	نظام غذائي
Bread	خبز	Dough	عجينة
Butter	زبدة	Dry	ناشف
Calories	سعرات حراريّة	Fat	دهن
Carrot	جزر	Fattening	مسمن
Cashews	كاشو	Favourite	مفضّل
Cauliflower	أرنبيط / زهرة	Fibres	ألياف
Charcoal	فحم	Fig	تين
Cheese	جبن	Fish	سمك
Cherry	كرز	Food	طعام
Chick peas	حُمُّص	Food consumption	استهلاك الطعام
Chicken	دجاج	Fridge	برّاد
Chocolate	شوكولاتة	Fried	مقلي
Cleaning	تنظيف	Fruits	فاكهة
Coconut	جوز الهند	Frying pan	مقلاية
Coffee	قهوة	Full	مليء/كامل

Garlic	ثوم	Nuts	مكسّرات
Grape	عنب	Oil	زيت
Green beans	لوبياء	Omelette	عجّة
Harmful	مضرّ	Onion	بصل
Heated / Protected	محمي	Orange	برتقال
Hob	غاز	Oven	فرن
Honey	عسل	Overeating	إفراط في الأكل
Ice – cream	بوظة	Parsley	بقدونس
Jam	مربّى	Paste	معجون
Juice	عصير	Pastries	معجّنات
Lamb	لحم غنم/خروف	Peach	درّاق
Lentils	عدس	Peanuts	فول سوداني
Lettuce	خسّ	Pear	إجاص
Limit	حدّ	Peas	بزالية / بازلاّ
Main dish	الصحن الرئيسي	Pepper	فلفل
Margarine	سمن صناعي	Pickle	مخلّل
Market	سوق	Pine seeds	صنوبر
Meal	وجبة	Pineapple	أناناس
Meat	لحم	Pistachio	فستق حلبي
Melon	بطّيخ	Plum	خوخ
Milk	حليب	Potato	بطاطا
Mineral water	مياه معدنيّة	Prawn	القريدس
Mint	نعناع	Prevention	وقاية
Miscellaneous	منوّع	Raspberry	توت العليّق
Mug / Cup	قدح/ كوب	Ready	جاهز
Mulberry	توت	Recipe	وصفة
Mushroom	فطر	Refreshing	منعش
Nutrition	تغذية/غذاء	Remark	ملاحظة

Salty	مالح	To drink	يشرب
Sandwich	شطيرة	To exceed	يتَجاوز
Sauce	مرق / سائل	To fry	يقلي
Saucer/plate	صحن	To grate	يبرش
Seeds	حبوب	To mash	يهرس
Sesame	سمسم	To mince	يفرم
Shopping	تسوّق / تبضّع	To peel	يقشر
Sieve	مصفاة	To prepare	يجهّز
Slice	شريحة	To roast	يشوي
Snack	وجبة خفيفة	To shake	يرجّ / يهز
Sour	حامض	To sprinkle	يرشّ
Spices	ابهارات	To stuff	يحشو
Spoon	ملعقة	To take/eat	يتناول/يأكل
Starters	مقبّلات	To turn	يقلْب
Steamed	مسلوق بالبخار	To use	يستخدم
Strawberry	فريز/فراولة	To water	يسقي
Stuffed	محشي	To whisk	يخفق
Stuffed food	مأكولات محشيّة	To wrap	يغلف
Sweet	حلو	Tomato	طماطم
Taste	يذوق/طعم	Type	نوع
Tea	شاي	Veal	لحم عجل
Teapot	إبريق شاي	Vegetables	خضار
Tinned	معلّب	Vegetarian	نباتي
To add	يضيف	Walnuts	جوز
To boil	يسلق	Water	ماء
To consist of	يشكّل	Well-cooked	مطبوخ جيداً
To cook	يطبخ	White beans	فاصوليا
To dissolve	يذيب	Yoghurt	لبن

HEALTH

Abdomen	بطن	Breast cancer	سرطان الثدي
Abortion	إجهاض	Breast-feeding	الرّضاعة
Accident	حادث	Bruise	خدش
Acupuncture	الإبر الصينيّة	Cancer	مرض السرطان
Addicted	مدمن	Cell	خليّة
Alcohol	كحول	Cheek	خدّ
Allergy	حساسيّة	Childbirth	ولادة
Amount	قِدر / كمية	Circle	دائرة
Analysis	تحليل	Circulatory system	الدورة الدمويّة
Anaemia	فقر الدم	Clinic	عيادة
Anaesthetic	مخدّر	Complaint	شكوى
Appetite	شهيّة	Consecutive	متتالي/متعاقب
Arm	ذراع	Cough	سعال
Artery	شريان	Cure	علاج / شفاء
Artificial	إصطناعي	Deformed	مشوّه
At risk	خطر	Disinfected	معقّم
Awareness	يقظة	Deterioration	تدهور
Back	ظهر	Diabetes	داء السكري
Beard	لحية	Diagnosis	تشخيص
Blood	دمّ	Diarrhoea	إسهال
Blood group	فصيلة دمّ	Different	مختلف
Blood pressure	ضغط الدم	Disability	إعاقة
Blood sample	عيّنة دمّ	Dizziness	دوران / دوخة
Blood test	فحص دمّ	Double	مزدوج/مضاعف
Blood vessels	الأوعية الدّمويّة	Drunkard	سكران
Brain	دماغ	Ear	أذن

Elbow	مرفق	Hearing	سمع
Emergency	حالة طوارئ	Heart	قلب
End	نهاية	Heart transplant	زرع القلب
Epidemic	وباء	Help	النجدة
Equipped	مجهّز	Hippocratic oath	قسم ابقراط
Experience	خبرة	Hospital	مستشفى
Eye	عين	Illegal drugs	مخدرّات
Eyebrow	حاجب	Illness	مرض
Eyelashes	رُموش	Immune system	جهاز المناعة
Eye-lid	جفن	In addition	بالإضافة إلى
Face	وجه	Incurable	عُضال
Fat cells	خلايا دهنيّة	Indigestion	عُسر هضم
Female	أنثى	Infected	ملوّث
Field	مجال/حقل	Injured	مصاب
Finger	إصبع اليد	Instructions	تعليمات
First aid	إسعاف أوّلي	Intensive care	عناية فائقة
Foetus	جنين	Joints	مفاصل
Following	التالي	Kidney	كلية
Foot	قدم	Knee	ركبة
Forearm	ساعد	Labour	مخاض
Forehead	جبهة	Lack of	نقص/افتقار إلى
Generalist	طبيب عام	Lecture	محاضرة
Hand	يد	Leg	ساق
Harmful	مضرّ	Let's go	دعنا نذهب
Headache	صداع	Life expectancy	العمر المتوقّع
Health	صحّة	Lightness	ضياء أو خِفّة
Health insurance	تأمين صحّي	Lips	شفاه
Healthy	سليم / معافى	Lung	رئة

10

Male	ذكر	Radiation	إشعاع
Malnutrition	سوء تغذية	Ready	جاهز
Manual pump	مضخّة يدويّة	Reduction	تخفيض
Measuring	قياس	Remained/still	ما زال
Medical	طبّيّ	Removed	زال
Medicine	دواء	Reproductive system	الجهاز التّناسلي
Metallic	معدني	Researcher	باحث
Minor ailment	وعكة	Salts	أملاح
Mix	ممزوج/مخلوط	Same	مرادف
Mouth	فم	Screen	شاشة
Nail	ظفر	Sex/gender	جنس
Neck	رقبة	Short sight	قصر نظر
Nerve	عصب	Should/ to have to	يجب
Newly born child	مولود	Shoulder	كتف
Nice / nicest	طيّب / أطيب	Side effects	آثار جانبيّة
Normal	طبيعي/عادي	Sight	بصر
Nose	أنف	Skilful	ماهر
Operation	عمليّة	Skin	جلد
Opposite	ضدّ/ عكس	Skull	جمجمة
Organic/ natural	طبيعي	Smoking	تدخين
Over drinking	إفراط في الشراب	Solution	محلول
Pain	ألم	Specialist	أخصّائي
Pale	شاحب	Spine	عمود الفقري
Pharmacist/chemist	صيدلي	Spread	انتشار
Pharmacy	صيدليّة	Steadily	مستمّر
Pregnancy	حمل	Sterilization	تعقيم
Preparation	تحضير	Stethoscope	سمّاعة الأذن
Prevention	وقاية	Suffering	إصابة

Surgery	جراحة	To miss out	يفوت
Swelling	تورّم	To mix	يمزج
Symptoms	أعراض مرضية	To notice	يلاحظ
Syringe	إبرة	To open	يفتتح / يفتح
Thigh	فخذ	To point to	يشير إلى
Thumb	إبهام اليد	To probe	يحرّض
Tip	طرف	To protect	يحمي
Tissues	أنسجة	To push	يدفع
To advise	ينصح	To reduce	يخفّف / يخفض
To announce	يعلن	To result from	ينتج عن
To be treated	يتداوى	To save	ينقذ
To blow	ينفخ	To stress	يثقّل / يشدّد
To breast-feed	يرضع	To stretch	يَمد / يمدد / يبسط
To breathe	يتنفّس	To suspect	يشُكُّ
To call	يطلب	To think	يعتقد / يفكّر
To check	يفحص	To transplant	يزْدرع
To close	يغلق	Toe	إصبع القدم
To cure	يشفي	Tongue	لسان
To diagnose	يشخّص	Tranquilizer	مُهدّئ
To die	يموت	Treatment	علاج
To disturb	يزعج	Trunk	جذع
To do / carry out	يجري	Urinary system	الجهاز البولي
To draw attention	يلفت	Vaccination	لقاح
To faint	يغيب عن الوعي	Vein	وريد
To feel	يشعر	Visit	زيارة
To forget	ينسى	Waiting room	غرفة الإنتظار
To hand	يسلّم	Ward	قسم
To include	يتضمّن	X-ray	أشعّة

TRANSPORT, TRAVEL AND TOURISM

Accent	لهجة	Delicious	شهيّ/طيّب
Affection	حنان	Departure	مغادرة
Airplane	طائرة	Deposit	عربون
Airport	مطار	Deprivation	حرمان
Application	إستمارة	Don't cross	لا تعبر
Arrival	وصول	Double	مثنّى/ ضعف
Available	متوفّر	Dream	حلم
Backward	إلى الوراء	Driving license	رخصة قيادة
Bad	سيّء/ عاطل	Eastern	شرقي
Balcony	شرفة	Enjoyment	تسليّة / ترفيه
Beat	إيقاع	Event	حادثة
Book/reserve	يحجز	Excel in / good at	يجيد في
Call	نداء	Exit	مخرج
Capital city	عاصمة	Forward	إلى الأمام
Car	سيّارة	Free time	أوقات فراغ
Care	رعاية	Full	عامر / مليء
Carrier	حمّال	Gate	بوّابة
Coach	حافلة	Good looking	حسن المظهر
Common / popular	شائع	Guide	دليل
Conversation	حوار/محادثة	Holiday	إجازة/عطلة
Corner	زاوية	Hotel	فندق
Courtesy	مجاملة/أدب	Humble	متواضع
Curve	منحنى	Independence	استقلاليّة
Customs	جمارك	Instead of	بدلاً من
Dead end	طريق مسدود	Instinct	غريزة
Decade	عقد	Issue	مسألة

Just about to	أوشك	Shopping centre	مركز تسوّق
Laziness	كسل	Side road	طريق فرعي
Loud	صاخب	Sight / scene	منظر
Luggage	أمتعة	Single	مفرد
Main road	طريق عام	Souvenir	تذكار
Meter	عدّاد	Speed	سرعة
Mobile	جوّال	Square	ساحة
More prone to	أكثر عرضة	Station	محطة
Motorway	طريق سريع	Suddenly	فجأةً
Moving	متنقّل	Surely	لا بد
My pleasure	سروري	Taxi meter	عدّاد الأجرة
Pavement	رصيف	Tendency	ميل
Peaceful / silence	هدوء	There is no doubt	لا شكّ
Police officer	ضابط شرطة	Ticket	بطاقة
Popularity	شهرة	Time difference	فرق الوقت
Post office	مكتب البريد	To happen	يحصل
Procedure	إجراء	To run	يركض/ يجري
Reasonable	معقول	To achieve	ينجز
Reputation	سمعة	To be courteous to	يجامل
Reservation	حجز	To benefit	ينفع
Responsibility	مسؤولية	To catch	يقبض
Risk	مجازفة	To contain	يحتوي
Road	شارع	To continue	يستمر/ يواصل
Road block	حاجز	To contribute	يساهم
Round about	دوّار	To cross the street	يعبر الشارع
Route / path	طريق / درب	To discover	يكتشف
Seatbelt	حزام الأمان	To distract	يلهي
Shop	حانوت/ دكان	To expose	يفضح

To fall	يسقط/ يقع
To find	يجد
To fly	يحلّق / يطير
To gain	يكتسب
To give	يعطي
To help	يساعد
To hide	يخفي
To hire/rent	يستأجر
To hunt	يصطاد
To inform	يخبر / يُعلم
To interrupt	يقاطع
To know	يدري
To miss	يشتاق
To originate	يتنشئ
To overcome	يقاوم
To pitch	ينصب
To prepare	يُعّد/يهيّء
To present	يؤدي / يقدّم
To reply	يردّ
To run	يركض/ يجري
To scream	يصيح
To shake hands	يصافح
To shock	يصدم
To spoil	ينغص/ يُفسد
To start	ينطلق
To surprise	يفاجئ
To try	يحاول / يُحاكم
To use	يستخدم

To wait for	ينتظر من
To walk	يسير / يمشي
To want	يريد
To wonder	يتعجّب/ يتساءل
Too much love	الحب الزائد
Tourism	سياحة
Tourist	سائح
Tourist guide	دليل سياحي
Tower	برج
Town	مدينة
Traffic light	إشارة المرور
Train	قطار
Transit	عبور/انتقال
Transport	نقل
Travel	سفر
To turn left	يستدير يساراً
To turn right	يستدير يميناً
Underground train	قطار الأنفاق
Unique	مميّز/مميّز
Use	استعمال
Valley	وادي
Video tape	شريط تسجيل
Village	قرية
Visitor	زائر
Welcome	استقبال
Western	غربي
Wide / vast	واسع
Within it	ضمن

CURRENT AFFAIRS AND MEDIA

Ad campaign	حملة إعلاميّة	Media	إعلام
Advertisement	دعاية/ إعلان	Monthly	شهري
Advertising agency	وكالة إعلانات	News	أخبار
Announcer	مذيع	Newspaper	جريدة
Article	مقالة	Poster	ملصق
Audience	جمهور	Price	سعر
Black and white	أسود و أبيض	Product	سلعة
Broadcast	بثّ	Readership	قرّاء
Channel	قناة	Report	تقرير
Colour	لون	Reporter	مذيع/ مراسل
Consumer	مستهلك	Revenue	مدخول
Copyright	حقوق محفوظة	Schedule	جدول
Coverage	تغطية	Series	مسلسل
Customer	زبون	Society	مجتمع
Daily	يومي	Sound	صوت
Digital	مرئي	Television	تلفاز
Documentary	برنامج وثائقي	To distribute	يوزّع
Free sample	عيّنة مجانيّة	To educate	يعلّم / يثقّف
Freedom of press	حرية الصحافة	To express oneself	يعبّر عن نفسه
Image	صورة	To go on air	على الهواء
International	دولي	To influence	يؤثّر
License	رخصة	To print	يطبع
Local	محلّي	To publish	ينشر
Magazine	مجلّة	To write	يكتب
Mark, brand	ماركة	Weekly	أسبوعي
Market survey	دراسة سوق	Yearly	سنوي

Chapter 2:

Society

Social and family relationships,
Social issues, law and justice,
Youth concerns, sports and hobbies,
Leisure and the arts.

الفصل الثاني

المجتمع

العلاقات الإجتماعيّة والأسريّة،
قضايا إجتماعيّة والقضاء،
هموم الشباب والرياضة،
الترفيه والفنّ.

RELATIONSHIPS AND FAMILY

Anxiety / worry	قلق	Drawer	دُرج
Bachelor	أعزب	Dream	حلم
Bed sheet	غطاء سرير	Equality	مساواة
Bedroom	غرفة نوم	Expensive	باهظ الثمن
Behaviour	سلوك	Family	أسرة/ عائلة
Birth-rate	نسبة الولادة	Family ties	علاقات أسرية
Bookcase	خزانة كتب	Flat	شقّة
Carpet	سجّادة	Freedom	حريّة
Chair	كرسي	Furniture	أثاث
Child	طفل	Garage	كراج/مرآب
Comfortable	مريح	Garden	حديقة
Confidence	ثقة	Gate	بوّابة
Conversation	محادثة	Generation	جيل
Cooperation	تعاون	Guest room	غرفة الضيوف
Corridor	رواق	Hall	قاعة
Cupboard	خزانة ملابس	Home	منزل/ بيت
Cushion	وسادة	Housewife	ربّة منزل
Definition	تعريف	Kind	نوع
Depression	إكتئاب	Kitchen	مطبخ
Design	تصميم	Lack of confidence	عدم الثقة
Desk	مكتبة	Liberation	تحرّر/تحرير
Dialogue	حوار	Love	محبّة/حب
Dining – room	غرفة الطعام	Made from	مصنوع من
Divorce rate	نسبة الطلاق	Marriage contract	عقد الزواج
Divorced	مطلّق	Marriage rate	نسبة الزواج
Double	مزدوج	Married	متزّوج

Maturity	نضج	Spouse	زوج/ زوجة
Motherhood	أمومة	Staircase	سُلّم
National service	الخدمة العسكرية	Table	طاولة
Nightmare	كابوس	Teenager	مراهق
Oak	بلّوط	Tenderness	حنان
Opposition	معارضة	To achieve	يحقّق
Paint	دهان	To affect	يؤثّر
Place	مكان	To attach	يلتصق
Principles	مبادئ	To choose	يختار
Problem	إضطراب/مشكلة	To confront	يواجه
Psychological	نفسي	To create	يأسّس/ ينشئ
Puberty	بلوغ	To divorce	يطلّق
Quilt	لحاف	To forget	ينسى
Rebellion	تمرّد	To keep	يخزن/يواصل
Reception room	غرفة إستقبال	To marry	يتزوّج
Relatives	أقارب	To mean	يقصد
Responsibility	مسؤوليّة	To mock	يسخر
Rights	حقوق	To repeat	يكرّر
Rug	بساط	To respect	يحترم
Serious	جاد/ خطير	To wish/hope	يتمنّى
Shared	مشترك	Toilets	دورة مياه
Similar	مشابه	Values	قيم
Single	مفرد	Wall	جدار
Sitting room	غرفة الجلوس	Wealth	غنى/ ثروة
Size	حجم	Widow	أرملة
Sofa	أريكة	Women's rights	حقوق المرأة
Split-personality	انفصام شخصيّة	Women's role	دور المرأة

SOCIAL ISSUES, LAW AND JUSTICE

Ability	قدرة	Conviction	إدانة
Accused	مُتّهم	Court	محكمة
Admiration	إعجاب	Court of appeal	محكمة استئناف
Arrogant	متكبّر	Court meeting	جلسة في المحكمة
Attack	إعتداء/ هجوم	Crime /murder	جريمة/ قتل
Audience	جمهور المشاهدين	Criminal	مجرم
Awareness	وعي	Criticism	إنتقاد
Badge	شارة/علامة	Death penalty	عقوبة الإعدام
Bail	كفالة	Defence	دفاع
Balance	مكيال/ ميزان	Dialogue forum	منتدى حوار
Bias	تحيّز	Dignity	كرامة
Blackmail	إبتزاز	Directed towards	موجّه إلى
Burglary	سرقة	Double standards	يكيل مكيالين
Capital punishment	عقوبة الإعدام	Enemy	عدوّ
Case	حالة/ قضيّة	Equality	مساواة
Cell	زنزانة/ خلية	Euthanasia	القتل الرحيم
Chaos	فوضى	Evidence	أدلّة / دليل
Circumstance	ظرف	Evil	شرّ
Clear / exposed	واضح/ بيّن	Experience	تجربة/ خبرة
Committee	لجنة	Experienced	ذو خبرة
Comparison	مقارنة	Expert	خبير
Concern	اهتمام	Fine	غرامة
Confirmed	ثابت/ مؤكّد	Government	سلطة / حكومة
Contradiction	تناقض	Guilty	مذنب
Contribution	مساهمة	He has / she has	لديه / لديها
Control/dictatorial	سيطرة	Ignorance	جهل

Illegal drugs	حشيشة/مخدرّات	Painful	مؤلم
Innocent	بريء	Partner	قرين/ رفيق/شريك
Innocent victim	ضحيّة بريئة	Physical abuse	اعتداء جسدي
Inquiry	استفسار	Popularity	شعبيّة
Institution	معهد/ مؤسّسة	Prison	سجن/حبس
Intent to kill	قتل متعمّد	Prosecution	إدّعاء
Investigator	محقّق	Punishment	عقاب
Issue	مسألة	Questionnaire	استطلاع للرأي
Judge	قاضي	Rape	اغتصاب
Jury	المحلّفون	Reason	سبب
Justice	عدالة	Regime	نظام / حكم
Lawyer/ solicitor	محام	Relationship	علاقة
Legal	قانوني/ مشروع	Release	إفراج
Life imprisonment	سجن مدى الحياة	Report	تقرير
Majority	أغلبيّة	Responsibility	مسؤوليّة
Many	عديد	Role	دور
Mediator	وسيط	Security	أمن
Members	أعضاء	Sentence/ judgement	حُكم
Money smuggling	تهريب أموال	Sergeant	رقيب
Moral abuse	إساءة أخلاقيّة	Service	خدمة
Motive	دافع	Shariah court	محكمة شرعيّة
Network	شبكة	Sign	إشارة
Nickname	لقب	Statement	بيان
Noise	ضجّة	Suicide	انتحار
On oath	محلّف	Supreme court	محكمة عليا
Opportunity	فرصة	Terrorism	إرهاب
Organization	هيئة	To abolish	يلغــي

To accuse	يتَّهم	To make	يصنع/يفعل
To allow	يسمح	To make a decision	يتخذّ قرار
To appear	يبرز	To meet	يلتقي
To attach	يرفق	To object	يعارض
To be freed	يخلى سبيله	To pardon	يسامح/ يعفو
To be about to	يوشك	To plan	يخطّط
To be convicted	يدان	To plead guilty	يعترف بالذنب
To be jealous	غيوّر/حسود	To raise	يثير
To benefit from	يستفيد من	To repent	يتوب/ يندم/يتأسّف
To break the law	يخالف القانون	To return	يعود
To commit	يرتكب	To rise	يرتقي/يرتفع
To consider	يعتبر/ ينظر في	To separate	يفصل
To direct	يوجّه	To shock	يهَز
To envy	يحسد	To sue	يرفع دعوى قضائيّة
To execute	يعدم	To threaten	يُهدّد
To expect	يتوقّع	To tip the balance	يميل كفّة الميزان
To expose	يفضح/ يعرض	To try	يحاول/يحاكم
To extract	ينتزع	To use	يستغّل
To find	يجد	To win	يفوز
To gain	يكسب/ يربح	Trial	محاولة/محكمة
To get	يكسب	Unanimity	إجماع
To give evidence	يشهد/يقدّم أدلّة	Unnecessary	غير ضروري
To implement	ينفّذ	Victim	ضحيّة
To imprison	يسجن	Victory	فوز/نصر
To lead to	يؤدّي إلى	Violation	إنتهاك
To look	يبدو / ينظر	Warning	تحذير
To lose	يخسر	Witness	شاهد

YOUTH CONCERNS, SPORTS AND HOBBIES

Activity	نشاط	Invitation	دعوة
Amateur	هاوي	Isn't it so...?	أليس كذلك...؟
Announcement	إعلان	Lab coat	معطف مختبر
Apology	إعتذار	Laziness	كسل
Approval	موافقة	Leisure centre	نادي ترفيهي
Athletic	رياضي	Lending	إعارة
Basketball	كرة السلّة	Location	موقع
Blonde	شقراء	Locker	خزانة
Brunette	سمراء	Loser	خاسر
Call	نداء	Main	رئيسي
Cancellation	إلغاء	Medal	وسام
Club	نادي	Mental	عقلي/ ذهني
Colleague	زميل	Motivation	دافع/ حافز
Concern	إهتمام	My excuse	عذري
Concert	حفلة موسيقيّة	Neck tie	ربطة عنق
Crowd	جمهور	Opponent	عدوّ/منافس
Cup	كأس	Optional	اخنياري
Did you find...?	هل اكتشفت...؟	Physical	مادّي
Energy	طاقة/ نشاط	Prize	جائزة
Enthusiasm/ zeal	حماس	Professional	محترف
Facilities	تسهيلات	Promise	عهد / وعد
Football	كرة القدم	Purse	جزدان
Free time	وقت فراغ	Record	رقم قياسي
Hall	قاعة	Referee	حكم
Happy	فَرِح/ سعيد	Relaxation	استرخاء
Hobby	هواية	Sad	حزين

Scarf	وشاح	To give	يعطي
Skill	مهارة	To happen	يتحقّق
Skirt	تنّورة	To imagine	يتصوّر
Social	اجتماعي	To leave	يغادر / يترك
Socks	جوارب	To lose	يخسر / يفقد
Spectator	مشاهد	To mean	يعني
Sports star	نجم رياضي	To move	ينقل / يحرّك
Stadium	مدرّج	To play	يلعب
Suitable	ملائم	To pour	يسكب / يصبّ
Team	فريق	To practise	يمارس / يتمرّن
Team spirit	روح جماعي	To range	يتراوح
Tennis	كرة المضرب	To receive	يحصل على / يستق
Theme park	مدينة ملاهي	To reproach	يلوم / يؤنب
Tights	جوارب طويلة	To shave	يحلق
To admit	يعترف	To suffer	يتألّم / يعاني / يكابر
To beat the record	يحطّم الرقم القياسي	To surround	يحيط
To burden	يثقل الكاهل	To think	يظنّ / يفكّر
To confess	يعترف	To threaten	يهدّد
To contribute	يشترك / يساهم	To tie / To connect	يربط
To cut	يقطع	To win	يربح
To distribute	يوزّع	Tone	نغمة
To enable	يمكن	Tournament	مباراة
To end	ينتهي / ينهي	Track suit	بدلة رياضية
To excel	يتفوّق	Vest	سُترة
To find	يعثر / يجد	Volleyball	كرة الطائرة
To fix	يصلّح	Wallet	محفظة
To get	يستلم / يستقبل	Youth	شباب

LEISURE AND THE ARTS

Adventurous	مغامر	Enjoyment	ترفيه/تمتّع
African	افريقي	Exhibition	معرض
Alleys	أزقّة	Fabric/ cloth	قماش
Ancient	قديم	Feature	قسمة/ميزة
Arabic	عربي	Good condition	حالة جيّدة
Art	فنّ	Greek	يوناني
Astonishing	عجيب/ مدهش	Guide	دليل
Autumn	خريف	Harbour/port	مينـاء
Bone	عظم	Henna	حنّاء
Carnival	مهرجان	Heritage	تراث
Chinese	صيني	Historical	تاريخي
Cinema	سينما	Humoristic	مُضحك
City centre	وسط المدينة	Indian	هندي
Clay	طين/فخّار	Innovator	مبدع/ مبتكر
Column	عامود	Jewellery	حليّ
Concern / interest	اهتمام	Keen to	يحرص على
Contemporary	معاصر	Leisure	فراغ/ راحة
Countryside	ريف	Leisure centre	مُنتزه
Craft	حرفة	Listed	مصنّف
Culture	ثقافة	Literature	أدب
Definite	يقيني/ قاطع	Material	مادّة /قماش
Desire	شهوة / رغبة	Means	وسائل
Disappointing	مُخيّب	Metal	معدن
Dome	قبّة	Monument	نصب
Drawing	رسم	Mountain	جبل
Effects/artefacts	آثار	Museum	متحف

Music	موسيقى	Spring	ربيع/ نبع
New	جديد	Suburb	ضاحية
Opinion	رأي	Summer	صيف
Painting	دهن/ صورة	Tattoo	وشم
Persian	فارسي	Theatre	مسرح
Phoenician	فينيقي	To allow	يبيح / يسمح
Pleasure	متعة	To be bored	يسأم
Poetry	شعر	To carve	ينحت
Popular/public	شعبي	To create	يشكّل
Positive	إيجابي	To design	يصمّم
Precious metals	معادن ثمينة	To deteriorate	يتردّى/ يسوء
Printed	مطبوع	To establish	يؤسّس
Radio	جهاز المذياع	To expect	يتوقّع
Realistic	واقعي	To explore	يستكشف
Roman	روماني	To make / build	يقيم/ يبني
Romantic	رومانسي	To present	يعرض
Satellite channel	محطّة فضائيّة	To show	يبدي / يظهر
Science fiction	الخيال العلمي	Tools	أدوات / آليات
Sculpture	نحت	Type	نمط / نوع
Season	فصل/ موسم	Urban crawl	الزحف العمراني
Selective	إنتقائي	Utensils	أواني
Shell	صدفة/ قذيفة	Valley	وادي
Site	موقع	Valuable stones	أحجار ثمينة
Skill	مهارة	Varied	منوّع
Solid	صلب	Walls	جدران
Source	مصدر	Winter	شتاء
Spectacular	مبهر	Wood	خشب

Chapter 3:

The working world

Education and training
Employment, business and industry,
Information technology.

الفصل الثالث

عالم العمل

التعّلم والتأهيل للعمل،
التجارة والصناعة،
تقنية المعلومات.

EDUCATION AND TRAINING

Ability	قابلية / قدرة	Education	تربية
Absent	غائب	Effort	جهد
Accomplishment	إنجاز	Entry requirements	متطلبّات الالتحاق
Algebra	الجبر	Envelope	ظرف/ مغلّف
Biology	علم الإحياء	Eraser	ممحاة
Biro pen	قلم حبر جاف	Examination	إمتحان
Boarding school	مدرسة داخليّة	Experience	خبرة
Bully	منتمّر /مستأسد	Experiment	تجربة
Business studies	دراسة إدارة الأعمال	Faculty College	كليّة
Busy	مشغول	Gap year	سنة توقّف
Calculator	حاسبة اليد	Glue	غراء
Card	بطاقة	Goal	هدف
Chemistry	كيمياء	Good at language	يجيد اللغة
Compass	بيكار	Graduation	تخرّج
Competition	مسابقة/ منافسة	Graph paper	ورق للرسم البياني
Computer studies	دراسة الحاسوب	Higher education	التعليم العالي
Copy	نسخة	History	تاريخ
Dancing	رقص	Homework	واجب بيتي
Deputy's room	غرفة النائب	Independent school	مدرسة خاصّة
Design	تصميم	IQ	معدّل الذكاء
Desk	منضدة/مكتب	Lab	مختبر
Dictionary	قاموس	Leaflet	منشورة
Digital	رقمي	Lecture	محاضرة
Discipline	نظام	Letter	رسالة/مكتوب
Driving	قيادة	Letter / thesis	رسالة ماجستير
Duty	واجب	Level / standard	مستوى

License	رخصة	Summary	ملخّص
Manual	يدوي	Tape	شريط
Margin	هامش	Technology	تكنولوجيا
Mathematics	رياضيات	Textiles	منسوجات
Music	موسيقى	Timetable	جدول زمني
Occasion	مناسبة	To add	يضيف
P.E.	التربية البدنيّة	To ask	يطلب/ يسأل
Paper	ورق	To contribute	يساهم
Pencil case	محفظة أقلام	To do	يفعل
Physics	علم الفيزياء	To establish	ينشئ
Playground	ساحة اللعب	To fail	يرسب
Popular	مشهور	To forget	ينسى
Present	حاضر	To go up	يطلع
Principal's room	غرفة المدير	To graduate	يتخرّج
Profession	مهنة	To learn	يتعلّم
Protractor	أداة لقياس الزوايا	To manage	يدير
Reading	مطالعة/ قرأة	To memorize	يحفظ عن ظهر قلب
Recognized	معترف/ معروف	To produce	يقدّم/ يصنع
Science	علوم	To replace	يعوّض
Session	حصّة	To revise	يراجع
Specialization	اختصاص	To search	يبحث
Sport	رياضة	To study	يدرس
Staff room	غرفة المعلمّين	To succeed	ينجح
State school	مدرسة حكوميّة	Unable	عاجز
Stationery	قرطاسيّة	University Education	التعليم الجامعي
Student accommodation	سكن جامعي	Vocational college	معهد مهني
Subject	مادّة	Wrapping paper	ورق تغليف

EMPLOYMENT, BUSINESS AND INDUSTRY

Account statement	كشف الحساب	Candidate	مرشّح
Accountant	محاسب	Captain	قبطان
Accurate	دقيق	Career	سيرة نشاط مهني
Administrative deputy	المعاون الإداري	Cash	نَقْد
After hesitation	بعد تردّد	Carpenter	نجّار
Agent	وكيل	Cheque	شيك
Agreement	اتفاق/ موافقة	Colleague	زميل
Application	طلب	Committee	لجنة
Application form	استمارة تقديم/ طلب	Communication	اتصال
Appointment	موعد	Company	شركة
Approved degree	شهادة معترف بها	Competition	منافسة
Architect	مهندس معماري	Competitive/competitor	مُنافِس
Article	مقالة	Complaint	شكوى
Atmosphere	جوّ/ محيط	Concern/care	اهتمام
Auction	مزاد	Confirmation	إثبات/ توكيد
Awareness	وعي	Consequence	عاقبة
Bank	مصرف	Consultant	مُستشار
Basis	أساس	Consumer goods	مواد استهلاكية
Billion	مليار	Content	مضمون
Black market	سوق سوداء	Contract	عقد
Branch	فرع	Contract conditions	شروط التعاقد
Budget	ميزانيّة	Contradicting	مناقض
Building	مبنى	Control	رقابة
Building complex	مجمع	Correction	تصليح
Business hours	أوقات العمل	Currency	عملة
Businessman	رجل أعمال	Current account	حساب جاري
Butcher	لحّام	Customer	زبون

Deal	صفقة	Expensive	غالي الثمن
Debt	دين	Experience	تجربة
Dentist	طبيب أسنان	Export	تصدير
Description	وصف	Factory	مصنع/ معمل
Design	تصميم	Failure	فشل
Developed	متطوّر	First round	الدورة الأولى
Development	تنمية/ تطوّر	Football player	لاعب كرة قدم
Development goal	هدف تنموي	Friend	صديق
Dialogue	محاورة	Globalisation	عولمة
Dimension	حجم/ بُعد	Good management	حسن التدبير
Dire need	أمَسّ الحاجة	Greed	طمع/ جشع
Director	مخرج/ مدير	Group	فئة / جماعة
Disagreement	خلاف	Hairdresser	مصفِّف شعر
Disappointment	إحباط /خيبة	Headquarter	مقرّ رئيسي
Discussion	مناقشة	Hostess	مضيفة
Disturbance	اضطراب/إنزعاج	Huge	هائل / ضخم
Doctor	طبيب	Import	استيراد
Editor	محرّر	Important	مهِمّ
Employee	موظّف	Improvement	تطوير/ تحسين
Employer	رب العمل	In line	مواكب
Employment application	طلب عمل	Income	دخل
Employment market	سوق العمل	Incorrect/false	غلط
Engineer	مهندس/ تقني	Industry	صناعة
Equipment	جهاز	Institute	مؤسَّسة
Estimation	تقدير	Interest	رِبَا /فائدة
Example	مثَل	Interview	مُقابلة
Exchange	تبادل	Item	سلعة
Expense	مصروف	Job	مهنة/ وظيفة/ عمل

Job hunting	بحث عن العمل	Percentage	نسبة
Judge	قاضٍ/ حكم	Performance failure	إخفاق الأداء
Lawyer	محامي	Period	فترة
Limited	محدود	Period of time	زمان
Machine	جهاز	Pilot	طيّار
Maintenance	صيانة	Plenty	مزيد
Management	إدارة	Practical	عملي
Market value	القيمة السوقيّة	Preparatory	إعدادي/ تمهيدي
Marketing	تسويق	Pressure	ضغط
Matter	قضيّة	Printed	مطبوع
Means/method	وسيلة	Printer	طابعة
Meeting	اجتماع/لقاء	Production	إنتاج
Million	مليون	Productivity	إنتاجيّة
Money	مال	Progress/ growth	نموّ/ تقدّم
Monopole	إحتكار	Project	مشروع
More beneficial	أجدى نفعاً	Promised	موعود
Multinational	عالمي	Questioning	استجواب
Neglect	إهمال/ تقصير	Random	عشوائي
Nurse	ممرّضة	Reason	سبب
Office	مكتب	Receiving	استلام
Official	رسمي	Recession	إنحسار/ انكماش
Opportunity	فرصة	Reference	مرجع
Paper work	العمل الورقي	Related	مرتبط
Part	شطر/ قسم	Representative	مندوب/ ممثِّل
Participation	مساهمة	Resignation	استقالة
Partner	قرين	Respect	احترام
Payroll/pay sheet	جدول الرواتب	Result	نتيجة
Peer	نظير	Revenue	عائد

Revolting feeling	تقزّز	Talent	موهبة
Salary	راتب	Task	مهمّة
Sales	مبيعات	Tax	ضريبة
Salesman	مندوب مبيعات	Taxi driver	سائق سيارة أجرة
Savings account	حساب توفير	Teacher	معلّم / مدرّس
Scientist	عالم	Technicality	تقنية
Secretary	سكرتير/ أمين سرّ	Test	امتحان/ اختبار
Serious	جدّي / خطير	Theoretical	نظري
Share	حصّة/ سهم مالي	To a degree	إلى درجة ما
Shop	متجر / دكّان	To abstain	يكفّ/ يمتنع
Side by side	جنباً إلى جنب	To accept	يقبل
Slot	موضع	To act	يمثّل/ يعمل
Source	مصدر	To apply	يُطبّق/ يطلب
Specialized	مختصّ	To be about to	يوشك أن
Specific	معيّن	To be located in/ to fall	يقع في/ يصادف
Stamp	طابع	To be proud of	يعتزّ بـ
Statistic	إحصائيّة	To begin	يبدأ
Stock market	بورصة	To blame/criticize	يلوم/ ينتقد
Storage	مخزن	To borrow	يقترض/ يستعير
Strike	اضراب	To cheat	يحتال /يغشّ
Success	نجاح	To check	يراجع
Successful	متفوّق / ناجح	To consult	يستشير
Suffering	مُعاناة	To consume	يستهلك
Suitable	مُلائم / مناسب	To defeat	يهزم
Surgeon	طبيب جرّاح	To encourage	يشجّع
System	منظومة	To establish	يؤسّس
System	منهاج	To exceed	يفوق/ يتجاوز
Table	جدول	To expect	يتوقّع

To express	يعبّر
To go bankrupt	يفلّس
To grow	ينمو
To happen	يحدث
To indicate	يؤشّر
To link	يربط
To look forward to	يتطلّع إلى
To make redundant	يطرد
To manage	يدير
To meet	يلتقي/ يجتمع/ يقابل
To overcome	يتغلّب على
To pay	يدفع
To permit	يسمح
To point to	يشير إلى
To prepare	يستعدّ
To price	يقدّر/يسعّر
To provide	يزيد/يزوّد/يقدّم
To put in writing	يكتب
To raise	يرفع
To range	يتراوح
To receive	يتلقّى
To refund	يعيد مالاً إلى
To regulate	ينظّم
To rely on	يعتمد على
To rent	يؤجّر/ يستأجر
To represent	يمثّل
To respect	يحترم
To respond	يجاوب/ يرّد

To retire	يتقاعد
To save	يوفّر/ينقذ
To show	يُري/يشير إلى
To suit	ينطبق / يناسب
To suspect / doubt	يشكّ
To take into consideration	يراعي
To take notice	ينتبه إلى
To talk to	يخاطب
To think	يعتقد/ يفكّر
Tone	نغمة/ نبرة
Trade fair	معرض تجاري
Trade/ business	تجارة
Training	إعداد/ تأهيل
Transfer	تحويل
Type	صنف
Typewriter	الآلة الكاتبة
Unemployed	عاطل عن العمل
Unemployment	بطالة
Union	نقابة
User	مشترك / مستعمل
Value	قيمة
Wholesale trade	بيع بالجملة
Will power	إرادة
Withstand shock	يتحمّل صدمة
Work experience	خبرة عمل
Workforce	القوة العاملة
Workshop	ورشة عمل
Worried	قلق

INFORMATION TECHNOLOGY

Amount	قدر / كمية	Hard disc	قرص قاسي
CD	قرص مدمج	Host	مضيف
Chat room	غرفة نقاش	In comparison	مقارنة
Compatible	متلائم مع	Index	فهرس
Computer	حاسوب	Information	معلومة
Computer age	عصر الحاسوب	Information revolution	ثورة المعلومات
Condition	شرط	Innovation	إبداع /ابتكار
Connection	اتصال/ إرتباط	Interesting	مُمتع / مُشوّق
Connective	رابط	Internet café	مقهى الانترنت
Continuous	متواصل	Invention	إختراع/ إبداع
Continuously	باستمرار	Key	مفتاح
Credit card	بطاقة الائتمان	Keyboard	لوحة المفاتيح
Damage	عطل	Knowledge	معرفة
Database	قاعدة المعلومات	Laptop	حاسوب محمول
Dictionary	قاموس	Memory	ذاكرة
Digital	رقمي	Microchip	شريحة دقيقة
Digital camera	كاميرا رقميّة	Mobile phone	جوّال/هاتف نقّال
Directory	دليل	Mouse	فأرة
E-mail	بريد إلكتروني	Negative step	خطوة سلبيّة
Encyclopaedia	موسوعة	Network	شبكة
Energy	طاقة	On line	على الخطّ
File	ملفّ	Organizer	المفكّرة / المنظّم
Floppy disc	قرص مرن	Password	كلمة السّر
Flowing	متدفّق	Phone bill	فاتورة الهاتف
Generation	جيل	Pirate copy	نسخة غير قانونيّة
Graphics	فنّ الرسم البياني	Portable	منقول

35

Positive step	خطوة إيجابيّة	To dazzle	يبهر
Practice	ممارسة	To enable	يُمكن
Preparation	تهيئة/تأهيل	To establish	يثبّت
Program	برنامج	To finish	ينتهي
Receiving	استلام	To happen	يحدث
Repair	تصليح	To have / own	يمتلك
Scientific advances	التقدّم العلمي	To hide	يختبئ/ يخفي
Screen	شاشة	To invent	يخترع
Sending	إرسال	To log off	يخرج
Shopping via internet	تسوّق عبر الانترنت	To log on	يدخل
Sim card	رقاقة الهواتف	To need	يحتاج
Site	موقع	To object / disagree	يُعارض
Software	برنامج الحاسوب	To paste	يلصق
Space	الفضاء/ مساحة	To refuse	يرفض
Stage	مرحلة	To release	يحرّر
Steady	ثابت	To spread	ينتشر
Subscription	إشتراك	To start	يبدأ
Technology	تكنولوجيا	To store	يخزّن
To adapt	يتكيّف	To surf the web	يتصفّح الإنترنت
To adapt	يتهيّأ/ يتكيّف	Touch screen	شاشة اللمس
To allow	يبيح/ يسمح	To update	يجدّد
To apply	يطبّق	User	مستخدم
To be limited to	يقتصر إلى	User-friendly	سهل الإستعمال
To click on	ينقر على	Virus	فيروس
To connect	يصل	Vital	حيوي/ ضروري
To copy	ينقل	Welcome	استقبال
To crash	يتوقّف/ يتحطّم	Word processor	المعالج
To cut and paste	يقطع و يُلصق	World wide Web	الشبكة العالميّة

Chapter 4:

The Environment and citizenship

Energy, pollution and the environment,
Campaigning organizations and charities,
Politics and citizenship.

الفصل الرابع

البيئة والمواطنة

الطاقة، التلوّث والبيئة،
الجمعيّات الخيريّة،
السياسة والمواطنة.

ENERGY, POLLUTION AND THE ENVIRONMENT

Acid rain	مطر حامض	Crude oil	نفط الخام
Action	فعل /عمل	Desertification	تصحّر
Air freshener	عطر تلطيف الجوّ	Disaster	كارثة
Allowed	مسموح	Dryness	جفاف
Asthma	الرَّبو	Ecology	علم البيئة
Average	معدّل	Electric power	الطاقة الكهربائيّة
Biodegradable	قابل للتحلّل	Element	عنصر
Bromide	البروميد	Energy	طاقة
Car exhaust	عادم السيارة	Energy lines	خطوط الطاقة
Carbon dioxide	ثاني أوكسيد الكاربون	Energy saving	توفير الطاقة
Cleaning	تنظيف	Environment	بيئة
Climate change	تغيّر الطقس	Factory	مصنع/معمل
Cloudy	غائم	Fertilizers	أسمدة
Coal	فحم	Flood	فيضان
Comparison	مقارنة	Fog	ضباب
Complaint	شكوى	Fuel	وقود
Comprehensive	شامل	Giant	عملاق
Conference	مؤتمر	Greenhouse effect	انحباس الحرارة
Confusion	تشوّش/ حيرة	Grossly abnormal	شاذ جداً
Container	حاوية	Hardness	صلابة
Contaminated	ملوّث	Health awareness	توعية صحيّة
Correspondent	مراسل	Health hazard	خطر للصحّة
Cover/packaging	غلاف	Huge	كبير /هائل/ضخم
Crisis	أزمة	Hydropower	قوّة كهربائيّة مائيّة
Critic	نقد	Inexhaustible	لا تنفد
Crop	الإنتاج الزراعي	Insect killer	مبيد حشري

Insisting	مصرّ/إصرار	Production	إنتاج
Insulation	عزل	Project	مشروع
Interrogation	استجواب	Quality	نوعيّة
Iodine	يود	Quantity	كميّة
Lack of	افتقار إلى /نقص من	Radioactive	مشعّ
Launch	إطلاق	Rain	مطر
Level	مستوى	Rain-fall	هطول المطر
Lie	كذب	Rainy water	مياه المطر
Local news	أخبار محليّة	Raw material	مواد خام
Manufactured goods	سلع مصنعّة	Reaction	ردّ فعل
Mistake	خطأ	Recycling	تدوير النفايات
Most appropriate	أنسب	Renewable	متجدّد
Most effective	الأكثر فعالية	Renewable energy	الطاقة المتجدّدة
National wealth	ثروة وطنيّة	Resource	مورد
Natural resources	موارد طبيعيّة	Rocket	صاروخ
Non salty water	مياه غير مالحة	Rubbish/waste	نفايات/هدر
Nuclear power	الطاقة النوويّة	Salty water	مياه مالحة
Nuclear risk	خطر نووي	Satellite	قمر اصطناعي
Oil slick	بقعة نفط	Scientist	عالم
Orbit	مدار	Sea condition	حالة البحر
Organic	عضوي	Seed	بذرة
Organic fertilizers	أسمدة عضوية	Serious work	عمل جاد
Oxygen	أوكسيجين	Session	حصّة
Ozone layer	طبقة الأوزون	Sewage	مياه البواليع
Planet	كوكب	Soil	تربة
Plant	نبتة	Solar energy	الطاقة الشمسية
Poisonous	سَام	Spring water	مياه ينابيع
Pollution	تلوّث	Storm	عاصفة

Sunrise	شروق الشمس	To mix	يخلط/ يمزج
Sunset	غروب الشمس	To negotiate	يفاوض
Thunderstorm	عاصفة رعديّة	To obtain	يحصل على
Tide	مَدّ	To occupy	يحتّل
To accumulate	يكدّس	To plan	يخطّط
To affect	يؤثّر	To pollute	يلوّث
To aim to	يهدف إلى	To prepare	يعدّ
To allow	يتيح	To put some efforts	يبذل بعض الجهود
To ban	يمنع	To release	يفرز
To be attracted to	ينجذب إلى	To replace	يبدّل
To be the best	يكون الأفضل	To separate out	يفرّق/ يعرّب
To choose	يختار	To spend	ينفق/ يستهلك
To consume	يستهلك	To suggest	يقترح
To contribute	يساهم	To throw	يرمي
To criticize	ينتقد	To waste	يبذّر/ يهدر
To disappear	يزول/ يختفي	Tornado	إعصار
To do	يقوم	Truth	حقّ/ صدق
To encourage	يشجّع	Type	نوع
To end	ينتهي/ ينهي	U.V. Rays	أشعّة بنفسجيّة
To estimate	يقدّر	Underground water	مياه جوفيّة
To excel	يتفوّق	Visible	ظاهر للعيان
To feel good	يشعر بالارتياح	Volcano	بركان
To follow	يتبّع	Volume	حجم
To happen	يحدث	Voluntary	طوعي/اختياري
To help	يعاون/ يساعد	Warning	تحذير
To hide	يختبئ	Weather	الطقس/حالة الجو
To live on	يعيش على	Well	بئر
To look after	يهتمّ/ يعتني ب	Wind power	الطاقة الهوائيّة

CAMPAIGNING ORGANIZATIONS AND CHARITIES

Absence	غياب	Fundraising	جمع التبرُّعات
Aggressively	بعنف/ بعدوانيّة	Glance	لمحة
Ambassador	سفير	Guilt	ذنب
Campaign	حملة	Help	مساعدة
Care	عناية	Homeless	مشرّد
Caused by	ناجم عن	Human matters	قضايا إنسنيّة
Charitable	مشاريع خيريّة	Injustice	ظلم
Childhood	طفولة	Innocent people	أبرياء
Conference	ندوة/ مؤتمر	International	دولي
Crisis	محنة/ أزمة	Isolation	عزلة
Criterion	معيار	Justice	عدالة
Deal	صفقة	List	لائحة
Despair	يأس	Long term	طويل الأمد
Destitute	معدم	Mental disability	الإعاقة العقلية
Developed countries	الدول المتقدمة	Misery	بؤس
Developing countries	الدول النامية	Need	حاجة
Disabled	معاق	Needy	محتاج
Disaster	نكبة	Old people's home	دار العجزة
Disaster victim	منكوب	Opportunity	فرصة
Document	مستند/ وثيقة	Organization	منظّمة
Donation	تبرّع	Orphan	يتيم
Empty	خال/ فارغ	Orphanage	ميتم
Exaggeration	مبالغة	Petition	عريضة
Exclusive to	مقتصراً على	Physical	بدني
Fair	عادل/ منصف	Poor	فقير
Feeling deprived	الشعور بالحرمان	Protection	حماية

Recent	حديث	To give time	يمهل
Rehabilitation	إعادة تأهيل	To hunt	يصطاد
Rich	غنيّ	To inflict	يصيب
Rights	حقوق	To leave	يترك/ يغادر
Security	أمن	To look after	يعتني
Shame	عار	To lose	يضيّع/ يخسر
Shanty towns	مدينة الأكواخ	To organize	ينظّم
Sponsorship	رعاية	To pass away	يلقى حتفه
Starvation	مجاعة	To protect	يحمي
Support	دعم/ إعالة	To reduce	يخفض
Tear	دمعة	To scold	ينهر
Terrible	فظيع	To shelter	يؤوي
Text	نصّ	To spread	يتفشّى/ ينتشر
To increase	يزيد/ يزداد	To surround	يحيط
To become homeless	يتشرّد	To take forcefully	يأخذ بالقوة
To become worse	يتردّى	To warn	يحذر
To beg	يتوسّل/يتضرّع	Torture	تعذيب
To blame	يلوم	Underprivileged	محروم
To build	يشيد / يبني	Upside down	رأساً على عقب
To compare	يقارن	Village	قرية
To consider	يعتبر / ينظر في	Volunteer	متطوّع
To debate	يناقش	Ways	سبل / طُرق
To doubt	يشكّ	Wheelchair	كرسي العجلات
To enjoy	ينعم	Will	وصية
To enlist	إدراج / يدرج	Work	عمل
To exceed	يفوق	Worldly matters	قضايا دنيويّة
To feel nervous	يشعر بالعصبية	Worry	قلق

POLITICS AND CITIZENSHIP

Abroad	في الخارج	Enormous	طائل
Absolute	مطلق	Ethnic	عرقي
Argument / debate	شجار/جدل	European Union	الاتّحاد الأوروبي
Award	جائزة / منحة	Expatriate	مغترب
Balanced	متوازن	Flag	علم
Ballot box	صندوق الاقتراع	Forced immigration	تهجير إكراهي
Bias	تحيّز	Formal/official	رسمي
Border	حاجز /حدود	Freedom	حريّة
Capital	عاصمة	Freedom of choice	حرية الاختيار
Capitalism	نظام رأس مالي	Generation	جيل
Circumstance	ظرف	Green party	الحزب الأخضر
Citizenship	مواطنة	Honour	شرف
City	مدينة	Identity card	بطاقة هويّة
Communism	شيوعية	Ideology	عقيدة
Complementary	مجمل/ مكمل/ متمّم	Immigrant	نازح
Contradiction	تضارب/ تناقض	Late	متأخّر
Cooperation	تعاون	Leader of the country	رئيس الدولة
Delegate	مندوب	Logical	منطقي
Demonstration	مظاهرة	Majority	أغلبية
Dialogue	حوار	Mayor	رئيس هيئة بلديّة
Dictatorship	ديكتاتورية	Minister	وزير
Diplomatic bag	حقيبة دبلوماسيّة	Minority	أقليّة
Early	مبكر	Most distinguished	متميّز جداً
Elected member	عضو منتخب	Nation	أمّة/ شعب
Emigration	نزوح	Nationality	جنسيّة
Enjoyable	ممتع	Origin	أصل

Parliament	مجلس نيابي	Suggestion	اقتراح
Parliamentary election	إنتخابات نيابيّة	Summit	قمَّة
Passport	جواز سفر	Temporary	موقّت
Permanent	دائم	Thought	فكر
Political party	حزب سياسي	To announce	يُعلن
Politics	سياسة	To attack	يهاجم/يعتدي
Position	منصب/ موقع	To be proud of	يفخر بـ
Power	نفوذ/ قوة/ سلطة	To be used to	يعتاد
Prevalent	شائع/سائد	To become	يصبح
Prime minister	رئيس الوزارة	To belong to	ينتمي إلى
Program	برنامج	To control	يسيطر
Racial	عرقي	To elect	ينتخب/ يختار
Rank	رتبة	To endeavour	يجرّب/ يحاول
Reciprocal	متبادل	To immigrate	يهاجر إلى
Referendum	إستفتاء	To include	يتضمّن
Relatively	نسبياً	To organize	ينظّم
Residence permit	إذن إقامة	To please	يرضى
Restriction	تقييد	To present	يقدّم
Role	دور/ وظيفة	To produce	ينجز/ ينتج
Rule/government	حكم/حكومة	To put an end	يوضع حدّ
Scandal	فضيحة	To resign	يستقيل
Self-capability	إمكانيات ذاتية	Traditional	تقليدي
Self-rule	حكم ذاتي	Tunnel	نفق
Sharing	مُشاركة	Varied	متنوّع
Socialism	اشتراكيّة	Violence	قهر / عنف
Speech	خطاب	Voting/ election	انتخاب
Stand for elections	يترشّح للإنتخابات	Work permit	إذن عمل

Chapter 5:

The International Context

Customs and traditions,
Beliefs and religions,
World problems.

الفصل الخامس

في المحيط الدولي

العادات والتقاليد،
العقائد والدين،
القضايا والمشاكل العالميّة.

CUSTOMS AND TRADITIONS

Adult	بالغ	Don't be surprised	لا تعجب
Advantage	فائدة/منفعة/ميزة	Dowry/marriage gift	مهر
Alternative	بديل	Elite	نخبة
Ancestor	سلف	Entertainment	ترفيه
Antique	قطعة أثريّة	Era	عصر
Area	رقعة/مساحة	Estimation	تقدير
Artwork	قطعة فنيّة	Etiquette	أدب التعامل
Awareness	وعيّ	Evening	أمسيّة/ مساء
Bond	رباط/سند	Exhausting	مُرهق
Built on	يقوم على	Expression	تعبير
Celebration	إحتفال	Extravagant	مُسرف/مبذّر
Circle	دائرة	Fancy dress party	حفلة تنكُريَّة
Civilization	حضارة	Folklore	فولكلور
Clan	عشيرة/جماعة	Harmful	مُضرّ
Cloak / gown	عباءة	Hate	كراهيّة
Consequence	عاقبة	Hesitant	متردّد
Continuous	مستمّر / متواصل	Hesitation	تردّد
Culture	ثقافة	Hidden	مخفي
Custom / habit	عادة	Host	مُضيف
Customs	جمارك	Human nature	الطبيعة البشريّة
Dance	رقصة	Inappropriate	غير مناسب
Dependent	معتمد على	Independent	مُستقِّل
Desire	رغبة	Individual	فرد
Dignity	كرامة	Inheritance	ميراث
Disadvantage	ضرر/ أذى	Institute	مؤسَّسة
Discussion	مناقشة	Issue	مسألة/ ظاهرة

Kiss	قُبلة	Sure/certain	مُتأكِّد/ متيقّن
Load	حمولة	Sword	سيف
Love	محبّة/ حبّ	The Arab gulf	الخليج العربي
Matter	قضية / مادَّة	The Middle East	الشرق الأوسط
Meaning	معنى	To agree/satisfy	يرضى/ يوافق
Minor	قاصر	To be afraid of	يخشى
Necessary	ضروري	To be annoyed	ينزعج
Norm	عُرف	To be good at	يحسن
Obvious	بديهي	To cross	يقطع
Odd	غريب	To envy	يحسد
Open	مفتوح/ منفتح	To fail	يعجز / يفشل
Optional	خياري	To hide behind	يختفي خلف
Personality	شخصيّة	To ignore	يهمل
Place	مكان	To limit	يُحدِّد
Problem	مُشكِلة	To make sure	يَتأكَّد
Pursuit	مُلاحقَة	To present	يقدِّم
Reason	سبب/ عقل	To repeat	يعيد/ يكرِّر
Region	منطقة	To sneak	يتسلَّل
Respect	إحترام	To spend	يقضي/ ينفق
Rosary / beads	مسبحة	To threaten	يُهدِّد
Sarcastic	ساخر	Traditional	تقليدي
Seated	جالس	Traditional dance	رقصة تقليديّة
Selfish	أنـاني	Traditions	تقاليد
Shaking of hands	مُصافحة	Tribe	قبيلة
Society	مُجتمع	Unnecessary	غير ضروري
Solution	حلّ	Useful	مُفيد
Specialized	متخصِّص	Visitor	زائر / ضيف
Strange	غريب	Wedding	زفاف/عرس

BELIEFS AND RELIGIONS

Ablution	وضوء	Discovery	اكتشاف
All year round	على مدار السنة	Distinguished	مميَّز
Altar	مذبح	Diversity	تعددُّية/ تَنوُّع
Ancient	قديم	Divine law	شريعة إلآهية
Angel	ملاك	Divinity	أُلوهيّة
Arc	قوس	Division	فرقة
Atheism	إلحاد	Expense	تكلفة
Before the eyes of	على مرأى	External	خارجي
Belief	عقيدة	Extreme/radical	متطرِّف/مُتعصِّب
Belief in God	الإيمان بالله	Fairness	إنصاف
Believer	مُؤمن	Faith	إيمان
Better	أحسن/ أفضل	Fasting in Ramadan	صيام في رمضان
Bottom	أسفل	Fate/ destiny	قدر / مصير
Buddhism	بوذِيّة	Features	سمات
Call for prayer	آذان	Forgiving	متسامح
Cemetery	مقبرة/ مدفن	Good ancestry	سلف الصالح
Charity	صدقة/ حسنة	Good deed	حسنة/عمل صالح
Christianity	مسيحيّة	Hell	جهنَم
Church	كنيسة	Hereafter	آخِرة
Citadel	قلعة	Hinduism	هندوسيَّة
Columns	أعمدة	Hope	أمل
Community	جالية	Hopelessness	يأس
Defect	خلل/ علّة/عيب	Huge	جسيم
Demand	طلب	Humane	إنساني
Devil	شيطان	Idol	وثن / صنم
Different	مُختلف	Idol worshipper	وثني

Imam	إمام	Physical	ماديّ
Inquiry	استفسار	Pilgrimage	حجّ
Insufficiency	قصور	Prayer	صلاة
Insult	إهانة	Praying at night	قيام الليل
Internal	جوف / داخلي	Praying hall	مُصلّى
International	دولي	Prejudice	أفكار مسبقة
Intolerable	لا يُطاق	Priest	قسّيس
Islam	إسلام	Prophet	نبيّ
Judaism	يهوديّة	Pulpit	مِنبر
Jurisprudence law	قانون فقهي	Rabbi	حاخام
Kindness	لُطف	Rare	نادر
Local	محليّ	Reincarnation	تناسخ / تقمّص
Manners	آداب	Religion	دين
Marble	رخام	Religious	متديّن
Materialism	المذهب الماديّ	Religious authority	مرجع ديني
Matter	مادّة	Religious sanctuary	ملتجأ ديني
Mental	عقلي	Rituals	مراسيم/طقوس
Messenger	رسول	Sect	مذهب/ طائفة
Minaret	مئذنة	Sign/picture	لوحة/ صورة
Miracle	مُعجزة	Sin	معصية/ اثم
Mixed	مُختلط	Soul	روح
Mosque/ Masjid	مسجد/جامع	Statue	تمثال
Norm/mode of life	سنّة	Stereotype image	صورة نمطيّة
Nun	راهبة	Strength	قوة
Offer	عرض	Stressed	شدّد
Orientalism	إستشراق	Success through guidance by Allah	توفيق من الله تعالى
Paradise	جنّة	Superstition	خُرافة

Period	عهد/ فترة زمنيّة	To prostrate	يسجد
Synagogue	كنيس	To provide	يُؤمّن
Temple	معبد/ هيكل	To spend	يقضي/ ينفق
To admire	يعجب ب	To swear	يقسم / يسّب
To avoid	يتجنّب	To take away	يأخذ من
To baptize	يعمد	To try your best	يحاول الأفضل
To become	يصبح	To turn to religion	يتديّن
To bless	يبارك	To wonder	يستغرب/ يتساءل
To care	يعني ب	Today/present	اليوم/حاضر
To come back to	يعود إلى	Tolerance	تسامح
To come to mind	يخطر على البال	Tomorrow/future	غداً/مستقبل
To convert	يتحوّل	Trapped	محبوس
To defame	يشنع	Type of	صنف
To deny	ينكر	Unacceptable	غير مقبول
To discuss	يناقش	Unfairness	إجحاف
To establish	يُرسّخ / يؤسّس	Unthinkable	غير وارد
To feel	يشعر	Untouchable	منبوذ
To guide	يُرشد / يهدي	Upset	منفعل
To influence/affect	يؤثر على	Useless	لا فائدة منه
To insist	يُصرّ	Valuable	ثمين/ ذو قيمة
To keep	يحتفظ ب	Verse	بيت شعر
To kneel / to bow	يركع	Verse from the Qur'an	آية من القرآن
To lead to	يؤدّي إلى	Virtue	فضيلة
To mean	يعني	Vision	رؤية
To meditate	يتأمّل/ يتفكّر	Weakness	ضعف
To neglect	يهمل	Wide	واسع / فسيح
To pray	يُصلّي	Worship	عبادة
To preach	يدعو/ يبشّر	Yesterday/ past	أمس/ ماضي

WORLD PROBLEMS

Abuse	سوء المعاملة	Exploitation	استغلال
Accumulation	تكديس	Explosion	إنفجار
Addiction	إدمان	Family income	دخل عائلي
Appalling	مروّع	Fatality	مُصيبة
Arbitration	تحكيم	Fight/conflict	صراع
Asylum	ملْجأ	Fire	حريق/نار
Attraction	جذب	Frame	إطار
Available	موجود/ مُتاح	Frustration	إحباط
Average	مُعدّل	Gang	عِصابة
Backwardness	تخلُّف	Hostage	رهينة
Beautiful	جميل / خلّاب	Ignorance	جهل
Boycott	مُقاطعة	Illiterate	أُميّ
Calamity	وَيْلة/ مُصيبة	Improvement	تطوير / تحسُّن
Civil war	حرب أهليّة	Infrastructure	بنية تحتية
Contraband	سلع مهرّبة	Issue	مسألة
Corpse	جثّة	Legal system	قسم قضائي
Crowded	مُزدحم	Limited income	دخل محدود
Damage	ضرر	Malnutrition	سوء التغذية
Deformed	مُشوّه	Management	إدارة
Destruction	دمار	Money laundering	غسيل الأموال
Dictator	دكتاتور	Motive	دافع
Dirty	قذر	Neutral	حيادي
Drowning	غرق	Obesity	سُمنة/ بدانة
Earthquake	هزّة أرضيّة	Organized crime	جريمة منظّمة
Eruption	ثوران / إنفجار	Outbreak	اندلاع
Ethnic cleansing	تطهير عرقي	Peace	سلام

51

Persecution	اضطهاد	To differ from	يختلف من
Prey	فريسة	To encourage	يحثّ/ يشجّع
Prisoner	أسير	To enjoy	يستمتع
Problem	مُشكلة	To exaggerate	يُبالغ
Property/quality	نوعيّة	To execute a plan	ينفذ خطّة
Raid	غزوة/ قصف	To exhaust	يرهق
Ransom	فدية	To exploit	يستغلّ
Refugee	لاجئ	To hear	يسمع
Remedy	علاج	To increase	يزيد / يزداد
Report	تقرير	To invade	يحتلّ/ يغزو
Representative	مندوب	To kidnap	يخطف
Settler	مستوطن	To listen	يستمع
Shameful	مُعيب	To overtake	يتجاوز
Siege	حصار	To perform	ينجز
Smuggle	تهريب	To reduce	يُخفّف/ ينقُص
Soldier	جندي	To refuse	يرفض
Stable	مستقّر	To struggle	يكافح
Support	دعم	To surrender	يستسلم
Term	مُصطلَح	To use	يستعمل
Third World	العالم الثالث	Touching	مُؤثّر
Threat	تهديد	Traffic accidents	حوادث المرور
To attack	يهاجم	Unparalleled	لا نظير له
To be forced to	يضطّر	Upbringing	تنشئة
To become easy	يهون	Uprising	انتفاضة
To become worse	يتفاقَم	Victim	ضحيّة
To commit	يرتكب	Violation	انتهاك
To conquer	ينتصر على	War	حرب
To deal with/ to treat	يُعالج/ يتعامل	Worldwide	عالمي

Chapter 6:

And finally...

Linking words,
Pronouns and interrogatives,
Names of some countries,
Opening phrases.

الفصل السادس

و في الختام...

كلمات ربط الجمل،
الضمائر وأدوات الإستفهام،
أسماء بعض بلاد العالم،
جمل إفتتاحيّة.

LINKING WORDS

Above	(في) أعلاه/ فوق	Between	بَين
According to	حسب	Between this and that	بين هذا و ذاك
According to	وفق	Briefly	باختْصار
After	بَعْد/عقب	But	إلاَّ أنّ/ لكنّ
After a while	بعد حين	By	من خلال/ بواسطة
Against	ضدّ	Certainly/indeed	مؤكّد/أكيد/قطعاً/ حقاً
Also/ as well	كذلك/ أيضاً/ كما	Clearly	بوضُوح
Although	مع أنّ	Consequently	لذلكَ
And	وَ	Contrary to	خلافاً لـ
Approximately/about	تقْريباً /حَوالي	Currently	حالياً
As	إذ	Due to/in view of/as	حيثُ أنّ
As for	أمّا	During	خِلال/ في أثناء
As long as	طالما	Either…or	إمّا...أوْ
As soon as	بمُجَرَّد أنْ/ ما أنْ	Especially	لا سيّما/خصوصاً
At a certain place	في مكَان مَا	Etc.	الخ...
At a certain time	في وقْتٍ ما	Even though/nonetheless	مع ذلكَ
At all	أبداً	Everywhere	في كُلّ مكان
At any rate/anyway	على أيّ (أيّة) حال	Except	باستثناء/سوى/ إلاّ
At least	على الأقَلّ	Except/save	عدا/ ما عدا
At most	على الأكثر	Facing/opposite	مُقَابل
Based on	إسْتِناداً إلَى	Far from	بعيداً عَنْ
Because	بسبب/لأنّ/بما أن	For and against	مع وضدّ
Before	قَبْل	For example	على سبيل المِثال
Behind	خلْف/ وراء	From	منْ
Below	(في) أدناه/ تحت	Hereunder	فيما سيأتي
Beside/ next to	إلى جانب/ بقرب	However	على كلّ حال

54

i.e.	أي	Or	أوْ/ أمْ
If	إذَا	Otherwise	وَ إلاَّ
Immediately	فوراً	Outside	خَارج
In	في	Over	فَوْق
In addition to this	بالإضافة إلى	Rather	بلْ
In order to/so that	لكَيْ/ كَيْ	Recently/lately	مؤخَراً
In other words	بكلام آخر	Since	مُنذُ
In spite of	بالرغم من	So that/ in order to	بحيثُ
In the beginning	في البدَايَةِ	Sometimes	أحياناً
In the direction of	باتِّجَاه	Still	لا زال/ و مع ذلك
In the end	في النِهَايَة	Such as/for example	مثلاً/ مثل
Indeed/verily/truly/yet	إنماً	Tantamount to	معادل لـ/ يساوي
Inside	دَاخِل	That said	و بعد هذا
It is a must	لا بُدَّ	The following	فيما يلي/ التالي
It seems that	يبدُو أنْ/ يَظهر أنَّ	There is no more	لم يعد هناك
Maybe/perhaps	ربَّما	Therefore / so	إذاً/لذا
Most of	أكثر /أغلب	Through	خلال/ عبر
No	لا / كلاَّ	To	إلىَ
No doubt/undoubtedly	لا شكَّ/ لا ريب	Towards	نَحْوَ
Normally /usually	إعتياديًّا/ عادة	Under	تَحْت
Not even	حتَّى ولا	Unprecedented	لم يسبُّق له مثيل
Obviously/of course	بالطبع/لا بدّ	Until/ even	حتى/حتىّ و لو
Often/in most occasions	غالباً ما	Where/ wherein	حيثُ
On	على	Whereas	في حين
On the other hand	مِنْ جهَةٍ أخْرَى	While	ريثما/بينما/أثناء
One of	إحدى	With	مع
Only	فحسب/ فقط	Without	بدون/ مِنْ دونْ
Only when	فقط عندما	Yes	نعم/ بلى

PRONOUNS AND INTERROGATIVES

I	أنا	Here	هُنَا
You (masculine)	أنتَ	There	هُنالكَ/ هُنَاك
You (feminine)	أنتِ	Who/whom (mas.)	الَّذي
You (dual mas. and fem.)	أنتُما	Who/whom (fem.)	الَّتي
You (mas. plural)	أنتُم	Who/ whom (dual mas.)	اللَّذان/اللَّذين
You (fem. plural)	أنتُنَّ	Who/ whom (dual fem.)	اللَّتان/ اللَّتينِ
He (masculine singular)	هُوَ	Who/whom (plural mas. and mixed)	الَّذين
She (feminine singular)	هِيَ	Who/whom (plural fem.)	اللَّواتي
They (dual mas. and fem.)	هُمَا	Who/ whom (plural fem.)	اللَّاتي/اللَّائي
They (mas. plural)	هُمْ	Is/are/do/does/did/ has/have/had	أ / هَلْ
They (fem. plural)	هُنَّ	Where	أيْنَ/ حيثما
This (masculine)	هذا	When	مَتَى
This (feminine)	هذِهِ	Who/whom	مَنْ
These two (mas.)	هَذان/هذين	Which/what	مَا
These two (fem.)	هَاتان/ هاتين	How	كَيْفَ
These (mas. and fem.)	هَؤُلاء	What	ما/ماذا
That (masculine)	ذلكَ	Why	لمَ/ لماذَا
That (feminine)	تِلكَ	How much/ many	كَمْ
Those (mas. and fem.)	أُولئكَ	Since when	مُنْذُ مَتَى

56

NAMES OF SOME COUNTRIES

Afghanistan	أفغانستان	Mauritania	موريتانيا
Algeria	الجزائر	Mexico	المكسيك
America	أمريكا	Morocco	المغرب
Argentina	الأرجنتين	Niger	نيجر
Australia	أستراليا	Nigeria	نيجيريا
Bahrain	البحريْن	Oman	عُمان
Bosnia	البوسنة	Pakistan	بكستان
Brazil	البرازيل	Palestine	فلسطين
Canada	كندا	Portugal	البرتغال
China	الصين	Qatar	قطر
Egypt	مصر	Russia	روسيّا
France	فرنسا	Saudi Arabia	السعوديّة
Germany	ألمانيا	Senegal	سنغال
Greece	اليونان	Somalia	الصومال
India	الهند	South Africa	جنوب أفريقيا
Indonesia	اندونيسيا	Spain	اسبانيا
Iran	إيران	Sudan	السودان
Iraq	العراق	Sweden	السويد
Italy	إيطاليا	Syria	سوريا
Japan	اليابان	Tchad	تشاد
Jordan	الأردن	Tunisia	تونس
Kuwait	الكويت	Turkey	تركيّا
Lebanon	لبنــان	United Arab Emirates	الإمارات العربيّة المتحدّة
Libya	ليبيا	United Kingdom	المملكة المتحدّة
Malaysia	ماليزيا	United States	الولايات المتحدّة
Mali	مالي	Yemen	اليمن

OPENING PHRASES

Here are some opening phrases to help you with your essay, speech or letter writing.

1) The introduction tries to place the topic concerned in context:

In the very first instance….	ولاً / بداية…
As an introduction to our talk….	كمقدّمة لحديثنا…
I would like to start my letter with…	أوّد أن أستهّل رسالتي ب…
Let's first start talking about…	سنبدأ أوّلاً الحديث عن…
Let's start our speech on…	لنبدأ الخطاب عن…
We will first begin our topic with…	بداية سنتناول موضوع…
The best way to start is with …	خير ما نبدأ به …
This essay aims to….	يهدف هذا المقال إلى…
At the start of the next millennium…	في بداية الألفيّة المقبلة…
I will try to clarify the reasons…	سأحاول أن أوضّح الأسباب ل…
We will examine the advantages and the disadvantages of…	سنتناول المنافع و المضّار ل…
We will present a burning issue …	نقدّم موضوعاً ملحّاً…

2) Different points of the essay may be put forward:

Here are the following points:	نطرح فيما يلي النقاط التالية:
First…	أولاً…
Second…	ثانياً…
Third…	ثالثاً…
We can also say…	كما يمكن أن نقول…
To start off let's examine …	فلنتناول أولاً فكرة…
To which can be added…	و إلى هذا نضيف…
To clarify the matter…	و زيادة في الإيضاح…
When did this issue arise…?	متى بدأت هذه المسألة…؟
The first question that comes to mind….	أولّ ما يخطر على البال هو…
How can we tackle this problem?	كيف يمكننا أن نعالج هذه المشكلة…؟
To what extent can we….?	إلى أيّ حدّ ممكن أن…؟
Is it possible to say that…?	هل ممكن القول أنّ…؟

3) Then ideas about how to solve the problem may be presented:

It is said that…	يُقال أنّ...
Some opinions are…	ثمّة من يرى...
In case of…	في حال أن...
To clarify this idea…	لتوضيح هذه الفكرة...
It seems that…	يبدوا أنّ...
This problem has its roots in...	تعود هذه المشكلة إلى...
The solution lies in...	يَكمُن الحَلّ في...
To start with we could…	بداية في وسعنا ...
To solve the problem we ought…	لحّل هذه المشكلة يجب أن...
One essential solution is…	من الحلول الأساسيّة ...
There is no doubt that the answer is	لا شكّ في أنّ الجواب هو...
I think the best step forward is…	أعتقد أنَّ أفضل ما نفعله الآن هو...
As far as …is concerned	بالنسبة لـ...
I think a suitable solution is…	أعتقدّ أنّ حَلّا مناسباً هو...
It is up to the government to…	يتعيّن على الحكومة أن...

4) A paragraph may usefully present another person's viewpoint:

As for the other viewpoint…	و بالنسبة إلى وجهة النظر الأخرى...
But in the case of…	أمّا بالنسبة لـ...
From another point of view…	من وجهة نظر أخرى...
In other words…	بكلام آخر...
Putting it otherwise….	بعبارة أخرى...
Contrary to what was said…	بخلاف ما سبق ذكره..
We can add to that…	إلى ذلك ممكن أن نضيف...
It is possible to say…	ويمكن القول..
It is impossible that…	من المستحيل أن...
On the other hand…	و من جهة أخرى...
The other opinion is…	و الرأي الآخر هو...
We have to oppose this view…	يجب أن نعارض هذا الرأي...
Contrary to popular belief…	بخلاف ما هو شائع...
Society cannot tolerate…	لا يستطيع المجتمع أن يتسامح مع...
It is out of the question…	من غير الوارد...

5) You may wish to return to an idea mentioned beforehand:

As mentioned earlier…	كما ذكر سابقا...
In connection with what was written…	بخصوص ما كُتِب...
Adding to what was said….	بالإضافة إلى ما سبق ذكره...
Related to the previous idea…	ربطاً بما طُرح سبقاً من أفكار...
Following on….	عطفاً على ما ..
Going back to the main idea…	و بالعودة إلى الفكرة الأساسيَّة...
Let's return to the point mentioned before…	و بالرجوع إلى النقطة التي أشرنا إليها من قبل...
To emphasize what was written…	تأكيداً على ما سبق كتابته...
To consolidate what was said…	ترسيخاً لما سبق قوله...
With reference to…	بالاشارة إلى...
As said previously…	كما ذكر آنفاً من حجج...
It is not enough to say…	لا يكفي أن نقول...
To stress what was argued …	تشديداً لما قيل..

6) And to sum up and conclude:

And finally…	و في الختام...
To summarize…	أخلص إلى القول...
To emphasize this...	تأكيداً لهذا...
And last but not least…	وأخيراً لا آخراً...
We can sum up what was said…	ممكن أن نلخص ما قيل ب...
All that was said points to…	كل ما قيل يشير إلى...
And in conclusion…	و خلاصة القول...
It is striking that…	من الملفت أنّ...
It follows from this that…	يتبع في ذلك أن...
After all arguments have been heard…	بعد سماع الحجج كلها...
The best conclusion we can draw…	أفضل ما يمكن أن نستنتجه هو...
Lastly…	و أخيراً...
All evidence leads to…	تشير الأدّلة كلّها إلى أن...
It is clear from all the above that…	من الواضح من كلّ ما سبق...
To conclude the essay…	خلاصة الموضوع...